Nazi Germany's Rocket Science: The History of the Third Reich's Experimental Weapons Technology and Research during World War II

By Charles River Editors

A V-2 rocket being fired during World War II

About Charles River Editors

Charles River Editors provides superior editing and original writing services across the digital publishing industry, with the expertise to create digital content for publishers across a vast range of subject matter. In addition to providing original digital content for third party publishers, we also republish civilization's greatest literary works, bringing them to new generations of readers via ebooks.

Sign up here to receive updates about free books as we publish them, and visit Our Kindle Author Page to browse today's free promotions and our most recently published Kindle titles.

Introduction

A picture of former Nazi rocket scientists at Fort Bliss, Texas

Operation Papercliip

After the last shots of World War II were fired and the process of rebuilding Germany and Europe began, the Western Allies and the Soviet Union each tried to obtain the services of the Third Reich's leading scientists, especially those involved in rocketry, missile technology, and aerospace research. Naturally, this was a delicate affair due to the fact many of the German scientists were not only active Nazis but had helped the Nazi war machine terrorize the world. At the same time, by the late war period, the Anglo-American Allies formed a clear picture of the Soviet state. Though forced to ally with the USSR's dictator, Josef Stalin, the West came to understand Communist Russia represented yet another hungry totalitarian power, and thus a very real threat to an independent Europe. British Prime Minister Winston Churchill realized the menacing character of the Soviets from the Katyn Forest Massacre of Polish army officers, if not before, while the Americans only gradually shed a naïve assumption of continued Russian friendliness after the war.

For their part, the Soviets retained ruthless imperial ambitions which manifested in various ways. They allied with Hitler for a time in 1939 to 1941, planning to divide Eastern Europe between their two expansionist states. They devastated the Ukrainian population with the Holomodor, an engineered, genocidal famine which claimed perhaps 3 million victims. The Soviet refusal to evacuate Eastern Europe following the war, instead retaining many formerly democratic countries as vassal states, spoke volumes about their intentions.

Both the Western Allies and the Soviets knew of Adolf Hitler's V-2 rocket program, the forerunner of ballistic missiles and the space race. Each recognized the immense strategic value of these technologies and wished to secure their benefits for themselves. As the Soviets contemplated additional expansion following the "Great Patriotic War" and the U.S. military came to understand the putative allies of today would emerge as the enemies of tomorrow, the men possessing knowledge of the V-2 rockets and other Third Reich military technology programs became seen as crucial pieces in the incipient NATO versus Warsaw Pact standoff.

The result was the American-led "Operation Paperclip" on the Western side, which resulted in German scientists putting their expertise at the disposal of the U.S. and other NATO members. Operation Paperclip aimed not only to obtain the benefits of German scientific advances for the United States but also to deny them to the potentially hostile Soviets, as General Leslie Groves enunciated: "Heisenberg was one of the world's leading physicists, and, at the time of the German break-up, he was worth more to us than *ten divisions* of Germans. Had he fallen into the Russian hands, he would have proven invaluable to them (Naimark, 1995, 207).

The Western approach, however self-interested, typically met with voluntary compliance on the German scientists' parts. In contrast, the Soviet answer to Paperclip, Operation Osoaviakhim, used the implied threat of imprisonment, torture, and death, the characteristic tools of Stalinist Russia, to coerce assistance from German scientists and engineers following the war. These men yielded rich dividends to the Soviet state in terms of achieving at least temporary technical parity with the USSR's western rivals.

To say Operation Paperclip had a profound impact on the Cold War and American history would be an understatement. The most well known example of the operation's "success" is Wernher von Braun, who was once a member of a branch of the SS involved in the Holocaust, would become known as the "father of rocket science" and fascinate the world with visions of winged rockets and space stations as a "new" Manhattan Project, one that NASA would eventually adopt. And in addition to the weaponization of ballistic missiles that progressed throughout the Cold War, von Braun's expertise was used for America's most historic space missions. NASA also had to develop rockets capable of first launching a spacecraft into Earth's orbit, and then launching it toward the Moon. The Soviets struggled throughout the 1960s to design rockets up to the task, but thanks to von Braun, NASA got it right with the Saturn V rocket, which to this day remains the most powerful launching rocket NASA ever used.

Nazi Germany's Rocket Science: The History of the Third Reich's Experimental Weapons Technology and Research during World War II analyzes the Nazis' technological advances and the covert attempts to import Nazi scientists after the fall of the Third Reich. Along with pictures of important people, places, and events, you will learn about Germany's rocket science like never before, in no time at all.

Nazi Germany's Rocket Science: The History of the Third Reich's Experimental Weapons Technology and Research during World War II

About Charles River Editors

Introduction

   Chapter 1: Developing German Rockets

   Chapter 2: German Aircraft Research

   Chapter 3: War Crimes

   Chapter 4: Destruction and Preservation

   Chapter 5: British and French Acquisition Efforts

   Chapter 6: The Soviet Union's Acquisition Efforts

   Chapter 7: Operation Paperclip

   Online Resources

   Bibliography

Chapter 1: Developing German Rockets

Though extremely different men in most ways, British Prime Minister Winston Churchill and Third Reich Fuhrer Adolf Hitler shared a passion for science, technology, and (sometimes impractical) "wonder weapons." In some cases, this fixation paid off handsomely, as in the case of British centrimetric radar, a compact, powerful radar type that enabled fitment to individual aircraft and contributed to the defeat of German U-boats.

Germany's science obviously failed to snatch victory from the jaws of defeat as Hitler fondly imagined it might. Nevertheless, the Germans made several crucial advances, including the first functional jet fighter aircraft, infrared sights for sniper rifles, plans for a "flying wing" style aircraft, nuclear bomb research, and V-1 and V-2 rocket technology.

Though some of Hitler's weapon programs inflicted damage on the Allies, most proved counterproductive from the Third Reich's point of view. They used up vast quantities of money, material, and know-how which otherwise could have produced large numbers of ordinary but effective aircraft or vehicles. In effect, Germany's experimental science programs hindered its war effort and produced advances whose benefits accrued mostly to its enemies, both eastern and western. The V-2 rocket even caused problems for the German food supply, since each rocket's fuel required the rendering of 30 tons of potatoes to produce sufficient alcohol.

Most spectacularly, the Germans laid the groundwork for the era of ballistic missiles to follow with the "Vengeance Weapons" program. The advent of relatively advanced liquid and solid fuels for rocket weapons made them viable again after a period during which rifled artillery overshadowed them. An additional factor creating German interest in military rockets came from their complete omission among the restrictions placed on Germany's army by the Treaty of Versailles at the end of World War I. This major loophole led the Germans to hope improved rocketry could replace artillery, which the Treaty nearly banned.

A V-2 rocket

The Germans also felt considerable popular enthusiasm for spaceflight, reinforced by the well-received 1929 science fiction film *Woman in the Moon*, produced by Fritz Lang. Max Valier, an Austrian author, also promoted spaceflight, interplanetary exploration, and spread knowledge of the potential offered by liquid-fuel rockets to an intrigued public. Thus, rocket science achieved both popular cachet and official backing in 1920s to 1930s Germany.

By contrast, Russian and American rocket scientists failed to drum up support despite their insights and advances. Robert Goddard launched the first-ever liquid-fuel rocket in 1926 but met only mockery and scorn from the press, which then ignored him. Konstantin Tsiolkovsky wrote extensively on the subject but achieved no acclaim. Ironically, both the Americans and Russians – who ignored their own rocket scientists earlier – embraced the German fad after exposure to Third Reich science in World War II.

Goddard

German rocketry continued to develop in the 1930s, largely driven by the inexorable enthusiasm of Hermann Oberth, who recruited the young Freiherr (baron) Wernher von Braun, a fellow enthusiast of the possibilities of spaceflight. An eccentric but highly motivated congeries of young engineers, scientists, and workmen came together to found the "Raketenflugplatz," or "Rocket Flying Plaza," the first construction and testing ground for modern rockets in the world. Eventually, von Braun's combination of easy, friendly personal charm and family clout won the rocketry enthusiasts Army backing and funding, albeit at the cost of secrecy and outside control.

Oberth

Von Braun

Rockets at the Raketenflugplatz

While most of the men felt patriotic and even nationalistic attachment to Germany, their motives centered mostly on being able to finally obtain the funding needed to create the rockets all of them dreamed of, as von Braun once explained: "There has been a lot of talk that the Raketenflugplatz finally 'sold out to the Nazis.' In 1932, however, when the die was cast, the Nazis were not yet in power, and to all of us Hitler was just another mountebank on the political stage. Our feelings toward the Army resembled those of the early aviation pioneers [...] The issue in these discussions was merely how the golden cow could be milked most successfully." (Neufeld, 1995, 26).

The "golden cow" gave much more "milk" following the rise of the Nazis to power several years later. While the army of the Weimar Republic wanted to restore German strength in case of an eventual war, Adolf Hitler and the other National Socialist leaders wanted swift revenge and immediate territorial aggrandizement. The strengthening of the Soviet Union during the 1930s also provided impetus to rearmament.

Eventually, the Third Reich's leaders chose the island of Usedom as the site for their rocket program. This elongated island lies just off the Pomeranian coast in the Baltic Sea, separated from the mainland by several lagoons. With beaches and the sunniest climate of any Baltic island, Usedom represented a popular tourist resort from the 19th century through the early 21st century.

The Germans built their rocket facility at Peenemünde, at the mouth of the Peene River, where

King Gustavus II Adolphus, the so-called "Lion from Midnight," and his Swedish army landed during the Thirty Years War. The coastal location enabled rocket tests without fear of hitting inhabited land, with ships dedicated to retrieving as much of various crashed rockets as possible from the Baltic waves. The remote location, chosen by von Braun, facilitated secrecy, while the generally clear, excellent weather provided ample launch opportunities.

Exploring new technical frontiers as they did, the Germans naturally encountered many difficulties, producing "duds" which led to better designs. Wernher von Braun remarked pithily about the first A-1 ("Aggragat 1") rocket that "it took us half a year to build and exactly one-half second to blow up." (Zaloga, 2003, 4). The final rocket received the designation A-4, though a half-size test-bed A-5 coexisted with it. The A-4 eventually received the famous designation V-2.

A fresh face at the V-2 facility in 1943, Dieter Huzel, described his first view of these futuristic weapons: "I saw them—four, fantastic shapes but a few feet away, strange and towering above us in the subdued light. I could only think that they must be out of some science fiction film—Frau im Mond [The Woman in the Moon] brought to earth. I just stood and stared, my mouth hanging open for an exclamation that never emerged. [...] They were painted a dull olive green, and this, said Hartmut, as well as their shape, had won them the nickname of cucumber. I laughed, and the spell was broken." (Neufeld, 1995, 10).

The Peenemünde facility eventually employed over 3,000 scientists, engineers, and artisans, plus numerous slave laborers. The brilliant Silesian chemist and rocket scientist Walter Thiel took a leading role, developing a highly efficient liquid oxygen engine for the A-4/V-2 rocket, an improved combustion chamber, better fuel injectors, and short, wide engine nozzles that together produced powerful thrust with maximum fuel efficiency.

Thiel

Von Braun, in the meantime, headed research on guidance systems, while continuing to serve as the rocket program's "face" and liaison with the military and government due to his persuasive, easygoing manner. Other men contributed depending on their expertise. Moritz Pöhlmann developed "film cooling" for the combustion chamber, using an alcohol film to insulate the metal walls so that the intense flame of the rocket engine did not melt them. Teams of engineers produced graphite fins or vanes for the rockets and precisely calibrated turbines to manage exhaust flow.

In 1942, the Luftwaffe started a second rocketry program, creating the world's first cruise missile (just as the A-4/V-2 represented the first ballistic missile) – variously known as the Fieseler Fi-103, the V-1, and the "Buzz Bomb." Each rocket had strengths and weaknesses. V-1s proved very cheap and easy to manufacture, but they moved slowly enough for aircraft to potentially intercept them and shoot them down. V-2s demanded immense expenditure to produce, but they moved so quickly no defense then existing could shoot them down. The Third Reich's leaders opted to fund both programs, though Hitler shrank from issuing a mass production order for the V-2 before it proved any exceptional usefulness.

A V-1 rocket

The Peenemünde engineers even prepared a preliminary design for an intercontinental ballistic missile (ICBM) dubbed the "America Bomb" or A-10. However, the technology for such a device did not exist at the time. Von Braun's scientists lacked the years of design and experimentation needed to produce such a long-range rocket.

In 1940, Heinrich Himmler, wanting to extend SS influence to the rocket program, pressured Wernher von Braun into joining the organization despite his lack of political commitment. Von Braun joined chiefly to keep working on his passion, rocketry, but his eventual rise to the rank of Sturmbannführer (major) tainted his reputation and dogged him following the war.

A few years later, Arthur Rudolph and several other leading Peenemünde figures began using slave labor at the facility in 1942. Contrary to their later claims that Himmler forced this move on them, their letters and memos at the time indicate nothing but enthusiasm among this group's members for the use of Soviet, Polish, and French POWs for coerced labor. Von Braun seemingly had no hand in the decision, but little evidence exists that it particularly distressed him, either.

Regardless, the A-4/V-2 proved to be spectacular during launch, delighting the scientists who labored so long to produce it: "'It looked like a fiery sword going into the sky,' team member Krafft Ehricke would recall years later. 'And then came this enormous roar. The whole sky seemed to vibrate. This kind of unearthly roaring was something human beings had never heard.'" (Spangenburg, 2008, 56).

The ballistic trajectory of a V-2 had an apogee of 58 miles and a maximum range of 200 miles. The rocket arrived at its target at 2,500 miles per hour, far too fast for aircraft or flak interception, and each missile strike came with essentially no warning that human synapses had time to respond to. Landing on open ground, a V-2 blew a crater 50 feet in diameter into the soil, while its mass and velocity permitted it to plunge all the way to a building's basement prior to detonation, demolishing even the sturdiest structures.

Charles Ostyn, then an 18-year-old resident of Antwerp, later recalled what the arrival of a V-2 looked like: "I saw this flash during the day, but only once – I just happened to look at the sky in the right direction. It was definitely not a contrail, but it was like a streak from a comet – as fast as a shooting star. It was a long, thin, white streak, more like a flash coming down to the earth. This was seen about 1-2 seconds before the impact. When a V-2 rocket hit in the city it was always followed by a huge black or brownish cloud of debris." (Ostyn, 2016, Web).

The V-2's accuracy remained very poor, however, with misses of up to 14 miles and sometimes as much as 40 miles not uncommon. The Germans built, at the highest estimate, 6,915 V-2 rockets, a remarkable and remarkably wasteful feat given the 46-foot length and immense complexity of each missile. Some 3,225 rockets that reached their targets killed 2,700 British citizens. The effects in Antwerp, however, reached appalling levels; as many as 30,000 civilians and soldiers died in V-2 strikes, including 591 people killed on December 16th, 1944 when a V-2 struck a packed theater, the "Rex Cinema," screening the Gary Cooper film *The Plainsman*. The rockets also sank at least 150 ships, and approximately 15,000 slave laborers died building the V-2s, a deadly effect which might perhaps also be counted among the weapon's death toll.

In the end, the V-2 provided an impressive display of technology's expanding potential, but it lacked the punch to achieve what Hitler wanted of it. Conventional warheads lacked the destructive power to make a limited number of ballistic missiles capable of forcing an enemy's surrender. Meanwhile, the German nuclear program remained so small that no chance existed of firing a ballistic atom bomb.

Chapter 2: German Aircraft Research

German scientists also worked on various aircraft and aerodynamics research during the war years, hoping to create designs capable of tipping the war in the Third Reich's favor. Precisely as with the rocket program, these efforts gave no tangible advantage to the Luftwaffe in most cases, but they provided a firm foundation for rapid aeronautics advances by the victors of

World War II.

    While the Allies produced some excellent propeller planes, such as the P-51 Mustang, P-38 Lightning, and Supermarine Spitfire, the Germans led in jet aircraft design and "flying wing" bomber design alike. Most never achieved reality during the war years beyond the planning and blueprint stage, but German designs enabled the Allied nations to jump ahead once the information fell into their hands. The British Royal Air Establishment (RAE) scientists A.P. Morgan and E.J. Davis stated, on seeing captured Third Reich jet aircraft plans, "We realized within a matter of minutes that our entire aircraft development program was already out of date." (Herwig, 2000, 125).

    In the final months of the war, the German scientists and engineers worked in a frenzied state to try to bring their latest designs into action and reverse the fortunes of war. The existence of numerous advanced test aircraft, captured, evaluated, and taken for study by the Allies, attest to this fact. Many designs achieved reality, but only as single examples or handfuls of aircraft still being test-flown by the Luftwaffe to work out bugs and design flaws when Allied forces seized the facilities.

    Some of the scientists and officers assigned to gather German devices and papers for study believed that the accelerated aircraft program represented a serious threat to Allied victory. Sobered by the speed and deadliness of the supersonic fighter and interceptor aircraft, equipped with jet engines, the Germans might have deployed in just a few months, these men reported that even a slight delay in the actual timetable of crushing the Third Reich might have proven fatal to its adversaries. The Germans drafted a profusion of designs, many intriguingly bizarre, but nevertheless, the ancestor of practically every advanced aircraft made following World War II exists among the blueprints of the Reich.

    While the reason for this advantage appears opaque at first glance, the Germans' scientific advantage over the Americans, English, and Russians resulted from perceptible causes. The other nations spent only stingily on their science programs, and in some cases neglected them entirely, as the derision hurled at Goddard's seminal first rocket experiment shows. They also set very limited goals, while the Third Reich, on the other hand, directed large resources to research and encouraged extreme, visionary, and highly experimental projects.

    Frank Wartendorf, part of the Operation Paperclip scientific advisory team in Germany at the end of the war, summarized this difference: "[T]here was no indication of the superiority of German engineers over United States engineers as individuals; rather, the improvements were due to more forward looking directives and freer purse strings for engineering and research matters. The scope of the German plans make it essential that our own plans be certainly not less ambitious in the light of our future security." (Hiebert, 2012, 288).

    The Manhattan Project provided confirmation of Wartendorf's proposition. The Third

Reich also possessed a nuclear weapons program, but the Germans gave it very scanty funding. As a result, it never developed beyond an amateurish, useless adjunct to the massively funded and ultimately successful aeronautics and rocketry programs (even if other nations reaped the success of that Reich budgetary munificence). Conversely, the Manhattan Project succeeded in giving America the first atom bomb due to the fact that the U.S. government pulled all stops in achieving its goal. The scientists received effectively unlimited funding, materials, and assistance to reach an achievable but visionary goal – and did so.

Driven by their passion for the scientific calling, the Reich's scientists continued developing and submitting new designs even as the "Gotterdammerung" consumed the Third Reich in spring of 1945. One of the last known designs presented to the Luftwaffe – by then a broken if defiant shadow of its former self – came from the drafting tables of a team headed by Professor Heinrich Hertel, working for the Junkers aircraft corporation. This aircraft, a flying wing design, featured a quartet of jet engines and a wingspan of 168 feet. With a top speed of 640 miles per hour and a range of nearly 11,000 miles, the bomber would carry 17,632 lbs of bombs (Herwig, 2000, 100). With the sublime confidence of a man of science, for whom the unfolding catastrophe of war sweeping over the dying Reich only represented a passing moment in human affairs, Hertel also included plans for a civilian version for transatlantic passenger flights following World War II's conclusion.

Hertel

Chapter 3: War Crimes

Excluding the anti-civilian use of Third Reich's aircraft and "wonder weapons" (echoed, in particular, by the British night bombing campaign and the American firebombing raids in

Japan), the Nazi science program conducted numerous war crimes. While the scientists did not participate in or order these actions, for the most part, neither did they object to them. Of course, the reality of resigning in a despotic system such as Germany of the 1940s also remains questionable.

The Luftwaffe effectively "rented" slave labor from the SS both to build facilities and to operate manufacturing lines making V-2 rockets and other high-tech weaponry. The SS actually charged a per-day fee for each slave worker, set well below the average wage of a regular German citizen, and provided all services, such as guards, food, and so on. Perhaps not surprisingly, the workers used for the programs underwent shockingly brutal treatment, regardless of whether they built V-2 rockets in underground manufacturing facilities or constructed wind tunnels in frigid, windswept alpine valleys in Austria. The SS preferred to spend the least amount possible on their slaves to maximize their profits, feeding the men very little, dressing them in thin rags, and providing no medical treatment. The guards motivated the victims to work with shouting, threats, and constant blows and beatings.

The most hideous events occurred at the Mittelwerke facility, built securely in a former gypsum mine where Allied bombers could not reach it. French resistance fighter, Polish soldiers, and Soviet prisoners of war made up the slave labor at the facility, which the Nazis deemed too sensitive to be handled by Jews. The Frenchman Jean Michel described the nightmarish conditions: "The Kapos [prisoner bosses] and SS drive us on at an infernal speed, shouting and raining blows down on us, threatening us with execution; the demons! The noise bores into the brain and shears the nerves. The demented rhythm lasts for fifteen hours. Arriving at the dormitory[...] we collapse onto the rocks, onto the ground. [...] Soon, over a thousand despairing men, at the limit of their existence and racked with thirst, lie there hoping for sleep which never comes." (Neufeld, 1995, 176).

The cold tunnels featured both constant moisture and incessant rock dust clouds in the air from expansion work. Due to insufficient water facilities, the men remained in a constant state of near dehydration, while the half fuel drums used for human waste soon overflowed. Men with dysentery, unable to crawl up on the barrels, were often beaten to death by the SS guards as they lay writhing in pools of their own diarrhea. Photographs from the Dora concentration camp, used to supply workers to Mittelwerke, show the usual rows of thousands of stick-thin corpses after the liberation.

These horrors underlay every V-2 that roared off its launch tray during the late war. While the Allies made eager use of German technology, gathering scientists, actual working devices, and mountainous hauls of papers and research literature with equal avidity, the stench of Nazi violence and war crimes hung about the projects. Metaphorically speaking, the Allies held their noses and proceeded regardless, making full use of the captured material.

The Soviets, of course, had no qualms about scooping up every bit of scientific data, every piece of advanced military equipment, and every scientist they could lay their hands on. Utterly unapologetic as ever, Stalin's agents eventually disassembled entire research facilities and factories for shipment to the Soviet Union, even going so far as to remove plumbing fixtures and other mundane objects.

While the democratic countries showed no greater hesitation in seizing the Third Reich's invaluable technical secrets, their governments needed reasons for bringing German scientists and technology to their shores. Given the understandable odium attached to Hitler's murderous regime, the matter required delicate handling and remains controversial even today.

Chapter 4: Destruction and Preservation

The Allied response to the Third Reich's advanced "wonder weapons" evolved over time. Despite efforts to keep them secret, the V-2 rockets soon became known thanks to the Polish resistance contacting prisoners working at Peenemunde. Initially, the Allies attempted no more than the destruction of the facility, plus various launch sites, with bombing raids.

The Western Allies soon recognized the extreme value of the Third Reich's scientific breakthroughs in rocketry and jet engines, however. As the Allies squeezed Nazi Germany back inside its own borders during 1944 and into early 1945, they realized that the Germans would likely fall before the Japanese. Accordingly, the Americans came up with the idea of taking and modifying German military rockets to aid in Japan's defeat.

This idea of repurposing V-2 technology to help with the struggle against the Empire of the Rising Sun sowed the seed that grew into the broader programs to follow. The growing realization that the Soviets represented another aggressive, dangerous military dictatorship soon added to the urgency and scope of the project. In that regard, the Anglo-Americans wanted not only to gain the Third Reich's science for their own use but to deny it to their uncomfortable allies from the east.

The Allies learned of the V-2 rocket program and recognized it as a serious threat in 1943 due to pieced-together information. A document that surfaced in Oslo referred to a rocket program; Polish prisoners communicated with (or escaped to join) Polish resistance operating near Peenemunde, providing a description of the work underway there; German prisoners made incautious references to the facility while speaking among themselves; and an analysis of previously ignored aerial reconnaissance photographs of Peenemunde revealed a probable missile base. The British increased their intelligence-gathering efforts and learned that the French resistance observed a number of large concrete rocket storage bunkers under construction in France.

As evidence continued mounting, the British convened a meeting of scientists and RAF personnel to discuss the matter. Some believed the A-4/V-2 represented a hoax, while others deemed it a reality, and the latter view prevailed at the meeting: "While… there may be technical difficulties in accepting the big rocket, there are even greater difficulties in accepting the big hoax.' It concluded that the evidence amounted to 'a coherent picture… The Germans have been conducting an extensive research into long range rockets at Peenemunde… Hitler would press the rockets into service at the earliest possible moment; that moment is probably still some months ahead." (Stocker, 2004, 12).

Shortly after the meeting, the British acquired a test-fired A-4 rocket that crashed in Sweden mostly intact. Unfortunately for the English war effort, the Germans used this particular A-4 to test the radio guidance system for the *Wasserfall* ("Waterfall") surface-to-air missile system, a completely different project. This led the British to conclude the Germans radio-controlled the A-4/V-2, prompting them to expend huge resources trying to jam hypothetical signals. In fact, the A-4/V-2 possessed no guidance system, instead staying on course through the action of advanced gyroscopes.

Operation Crossbow began as an attempt to disrupt the German rocket program with bombing raids. On the night of August 17th to 18th, 1943, 598 Lancaster and Halifax bombers struck the Peenemunde facility under a brilliant summer full moon, while a small diversionary raid towards Berlin successfully drew off Luftwaffe air cover. The British achieved total tactical surprise, setting much of the complex on fire.

In the mayhem, the SS guards machine-gunned prisoners who tried to escape from their burning compounds, lest some stage a breakout and bring news of the rockets to the Allies. Walter Dornberger, the general in charge of the complex, emerged in tunic and slippers to view the devastation even as it unfolded around him: "He was greeted by a scene that, he was to record, 'had a sinister and appalling beauty of its own.' Searchlights stabbed into a night sky full of stars. The smoke canisters surrounding Peenemunde had been set off [and] drifting clouds of mist now mixed with the brilliance of the full moon and the rainbow colors of the dropping marker flares. There were red tongues of roaring fire everywhere." (McGovern, 1964, 27).

178 German technicians and scientists died in the raid, along with nearly 800 slave laborers. One of them was Dr. Walter Thiel, the indispensible developer of rocket engines, who ran from his house with his wife and children and dove into a shelter nearby. Moments later, a bomb plunged directly into the shelter, blowing the entire family to smithereens. In one of the countless grim ironies of the war, their unprotected house stood intact and unharmed nearby except for broken windows.

When Wernher von Braun surveyed the facility from the air the next morning, he reported it resembled the cratered surface of the moon. This raid prompted the removal of the rocket program to various secret, mainly underground sites, inadvertently causing the subterranean horrors of Mittelwerke and its sister facilities.

Operation Crossbow strikes continued throughout late 1943 and through much of 1944. The bombers dropped 100,000 tons of bombs on V-1 launch sites and 20,000 tons on V-2 facilities, transport, and related infrastructure. Nonetheless, Operation Crossbow can only be judged a catastrophic failure in military terms, as the Allies lost 450 aircraft and 2,300 airmen killed in order to damage or destroy just 48 rockets out of the thousands launched.

The operation ended as the advancing forces of the Western Allies pushed into German territory, forcing the progressive withdrawal of the rocket units. At this point, also, the Allies began substituting an effort to capture Third Reich technology, rather than merely annihilating it.

Immediately before the D-Day landings, the Western Allies created a dedicated series of units charged with locating and retrieving German technological secrets in the territories soon to be liberated, and during the invasion of Germany. T-Force simply meant "Target Force." Approximately 3,000 investigators formed the core of the T-Forces, with attached units of British infantry and American combat engineers increasing the size of these detachments. The T-Forces answered to CIOS, the Combined Intelligence Objectives Subcommittee.

The T-Forces emphasized mobility and moved either just behind the fighting front or occasionally slightly ahead of it. Their role consisted in capturing and preserving installations of scientific or technological interest, and securing people with similar value. One of the T-Force programs received the candid name of "Operation Plunder."

Though the T-Forces consisted of armed men with some vehicle support, their main mission resembled a mobile security force rather than a combat unit. The orders establishing the T-Forces included the following description of their duties: "'T' Forces are, therefore, considered to be required to perform the following tasks: (a) Moving in the immediate wake of the assaulting forces. (b) Locating and securing intact the targets concerned. (c) Preserving them from destruction, loot, robbery and, if necessary counter attack, until the completion of their examination by teams of experts or until the removal of the essential installations or documents. (d) In enemy territory, providing armed escorts for the expert investigators."

The T-Forces needed to defend the technological and scientific assets not only from numerous bands of prowling Wehrmacht soldiers left in the countryside after the defeat of the main German forces in the area, but also looting soldiers of their own side and displaced persons. In fact, the T-Force soldiers soon came to view "displaced persons" as the biggest threat of all. Understandably, many released prisoners tried to take a futile revenge against the Reich by burning or smashing its abandoned facilities.

The T-Forces used armored cars and halftracks in their operations, and they occasionally found themselves in skirmishes with retreating Wehrmacht units or bands of German saboteurs. They also stumbled across various horrors left behind by the retreating Germans, including some of the smaller concentration camps.

In some places, such as Kiel, the T-Forces actually enlisted the Third Reich's guards and police temporarily to help protect vital facilities from arson or vandalism, as a British T-Force diary reported: "[T]he German military forces and police would be allowed to keep their rifles. [...] The police, evidently used to taking orders, were prepared to do anything ordered. Reports continued to come in to 'T' Force headquarters of German armed guards on certain dumps and targets. All troops were told to allow the Germans to carry on with the guards, which they were doing very well."

While modern sensationalist press accounts of the T-Forces stress their "Gestapo-like" "abduction" of German scientists, the vast majority of T-Force operations consisted of relatively mundane, though risky, occupation of factories and research centers.

The Alsos Mission involved T-Forces sent to track down Germany's nuclear weapons program, which the Allies believed much larger than it actually was. Colonel Boris T. Pash headed the first Alsos mission in Italy in 1944, while the Americans chose Samuel A. Goudsmit to head the second in Germany in 1945, largely due to his fluency in European languages, but also, as he noted wryly, because of his expendability: he possessed a background in nuclear physics but never worked on the Manhattan Project.

Goudsmit

A picture of T-Force workers working on a German nuclear pile in April 1945

The detective work for tracking down the largely nonexistent German nuclear project frequently involved risks, since it occurred in a war zone. Goudsmit recounted one of the many attempts the team made to obtain clues: "We had collected a few bottles of water from the river Rhine [...] Captain Robert Blake had gone on the bridge under fire at that dangerous spearhead in Holland late in September, 1944, and midstream had filled the bottles with the precious river water. We figured that if the Germans had a large atom bomb plant, they might be using the Rhine or its subsidiaries for uranium pile cooling." (Goudsmit, 1996, 21-22).

This clever bit of research might well have worked had such a plant existed, because trace radioactivity could be detected even by the laboratories of 1944-45. Carefully shipped back to Washington, D.C. for analysis, the Rhine water samples proved radiation-free.

The Alsos Mission eventually tracked down the Third Reich's trivial atom bomb research efforts through a long series of field investigations. During the course of these missions, Goudsmit and his team rounded up 10 of the scientists most closely involved in the abortive German nuclear program. According to him, the men's reaction when they first heard of the

Hiroshima blast while at dinner remained dismissive: "'It can't be an atomic bomb,' one of their number said. 'It's probably propaganda, just as it was in Germany. They may have some new explosive or an extra large bomb they call 'atomic,' but it's certainly not what we would have called an atomic   bomb. It has nothing whatever to do with the uranium problem.'" (Goudsmit, 1996, 134).

Goudsmit also claimed that when they learned details of the explosion several hours later, the scientists showed strong signs of despondency at the failure of their scientific program. While not impossible or even improbable, Goudsmit's clear and undisguised loathing for the Germans might have colored his recollection of their response.

Finally, the Americans started Operation Overcast to collect valuable German personnel and, hopefully, induce their immigration to the United States following the war. Though problematic and ultimately abandoned, Operation Overcast proved the precursor to the much more effective Operation Paperclip.

Many of the German scientists themselves effectively collaborated in transferring their discoveries to the victorious Allies. While Hitler, his military chief Field Marshal Wilhelm Keitel, and the SS did their best to destroy the information and machines created, many of the scientists worked secretly for the opposite result.

Caring nothing for politics and deeply passionate about preserving their creations for the general benefit of humankind, the Reich's researchers took considerable risks copying documents onto microfilm for later release to the Allies or postwar Germany, or concealing objects where they might survive the SS or vengeful workers. One of the scientists described the thought processes behind these actions: "We could not understand the senseless destruction of scientific equipment […] all efforts were made to save as much as possible of the work already done […] The development of high-speed flying bodies is one of the most urgent and most interesting technical problems of the near future. The destruction of the tool for this development and the destruction of his own brain work would actually mean the suicide of the scientist." (Hiebert, 2012, 291).

Material remained for the Allies to capture, in considerable measure, because the scientists themselves worked to prevent it from being smashed or burned. While many secrets also suffered destruction, due to bombing, combat, vandalism by soldiers or liberated prisoners, and deliberate destruction by agents of the Gestapo and SS, plenty of it survived, and the German scientists themselves, with their apolitical dedication to discovery, merit partial credit for that fact.

On March 19th, 1945, Hitler issued his infamous "scorched earth" orders, in which everything of any value to the Allies should be burned or otherwise destroyed, but Wernher von Braun, confronted with the likely destruction of 13 years of painstaking research, took action to preserve the vast quantities of priceless data generated by the rocketry program. Gathering 14 tons of documents, von Braun entrusted the papers to two men, Dieter Huzel and Bernhard Tessmann, whose loyalty he trusted implicitly. Together with seven soldiers, these two men drove a car and a trio of 3-ton Opel trucks in search of an abandoned mine where they could hide the precious documentation. The men searched desperately and finally found a pair of abandoned iron mines near the tiny town of Dornten. The nine men spent hours wrestling countless heavy boxes of papers into safety. Finally, Huzel recounted, the task ended: "Mission accomplished, and all of a sudden I felt dead tired. I looked around, and saw my weariness reflected in the faces of the others, leaning against the wall, squatting on the floor, or standing with hands on hips, covered with sweat and utterly disarrayed." (McGovern, 1964, 116).

The Germans dynamited the entrance and then left. Though the Americans discovered the hiding place within a few weeks, von Braun's actions may well have saved a large portion of Peenemunde's research from Hitler's destruction order.

Chapter 5: British and French Acquisition Efforts

The Allies pressed every form of transportation available into service for hauling off their immense war prizes, including aircraft, trucks, and railways. Both the Soviets and the Western Allies disassembled entire scientific and manufacturing facilities and moved them to their own countries, rebuilding the structures at carefully selected sites. In some cases, these facilities proved the source of disputes, while in others, British, American, French, or Soviet teams secured troves of information, machinery, and structures without interference from other searchers.

Sir Roy Fedden headed the British team sent to defeated Germany by Sir Stafford Cripps. Fedden, a slim, elegant, clean-shaven man whose photographs usually reveal an expression of focused determination, showed keen intelligence and a fascination with car and aircraft engines at an early age. Passionately fond of his wife Norah Crew, and somehow finding time between engine experiments to sail and fish, Fedden, 60 years of age in 1945, attacked his task with customary gusto.

Fedden

Years earlier, Erhardt Milch and Hermann Goering, to Fedden's astonishment, permitted him to tour no less than 17 of their secret aeronautics facilities when he visited Germany in 1937 and 1938. The Luftwaffe leaders hoped to overawe Fedden with the potential of German military aircraft design, and thus cause him to influence the British government to reach an accommodation with the Third Reich. Fedden, in fact, urged the English leadership to modernize their aircraft design to match the Germans' potential and was fired.

Realizing their error several years later, the government re-employed Fedden in 1944, and a mix of aeronautics engineers, scientists, and RAF officers comprised Fedden's team. The men left England on June 12th, 1945 aboard two Douglas C-47 Skytrain transport aircraft acquired through Lend-Lease and given the designation "Dakota" by the RAF. Fedden already appreciated German engine and aircraft design, and had a brief to secure jet engines as the first priority,

The team's first stop in the defeated, crater-pocked Reich consisted of the massive Hermann Goering Institute at Volkenrode, a Luftwaffe complex featuring laboratories, advanced production facilities and workshops, and various testing buildings. The Hermann Goering

Institute remained intact until the war's end because the Germans had successfully camouflaged it, despite the complex covering 1,000 acres. The buildings featured a scattered, random arrangement on partially forested land to resemble villages to aerial reconnaissance.

Since a large highway would point unmistakeably to a facility, the Germans built a huge tunnel from the city of Braunschweig to Volkenrode to transport in vehicles, materials, fuel, and supplies on a massive scale invisible from above ground. As a final detail, the Institute's airstrip blended a checkerboard of tarmac and mixed grass plantings, producing a surface suitable for aircraft but completely disguising the telltale outline from the air. The Institute's camouflage itself constituted a notable achievement; only when American infantry soldiers actually passed across the site did they identify it.

This complex – dubbed in honor of the corpulent, coarse, fiery head of the Luftwaffe – actually lay in the Russian occupation zone laid out at the Yalta conference, but the American military forces had crashed powerfully through withering Wehrmacht opposition to establish a front line 200 miles eastward. Fedden's task therefore consisted of removing everything of value from the Institute before the Soviets occupied the area.

The Americans naturally made full use of their access to the site before Fedden arrived. George S. Schairer, a Boeing aerodynamics scientist accompanying the American military's scientific mission in Germany, wrote to Benjamin Cohn from Volkenrode on May 10th, 1945, about Third Reich aircraft design technology. He noted that the Germans "are ahead of us on a few items [...] The Germans have been doing extensive work on high speed aerodynamics. This has led to one very important discovery. Sweepback or sweepforward has a very large effect on critical Mach No. [...] The   flow parallel to the wing cannot [affect] the critical Mach No. [...] A certain amount of experimental proof exists for this sweepback effect." (Boyne, 2007, 72). His letter, together with the documents he collected, resulted directly in a sophisticated swept-wing design appearing on both the Boeing B-47 Stratojet strategic bomber and the superb North American F-86 Sabre jet fighter.

The Boeing B-47 Stratojet strategic bomber

An F-86 Sabre

Fedden commented tartly on how the Americans "were making themselves at home" when he arrived. In fact, the Americans found the watchful British "crimped their style," but they still managed to secure some material for their own nation. The leader of the American mission, Donald Putt, described his technique: "I had a little airline of my own, one B-24 and one B-17. The trick was to get whatever test equipment and documentation out of the place without the British noticing. As soon as everybody was in bed and the lights were out, we'd spring into action. There was an airfield just across town, and with trucks we'd haul this stuff over there, and quickly load it on my B-17 or B-24. [...] This went on for some time until the British caught on." (Samuel, 2004, 155).

Fedden clearly understood the value of this facility and the technological secrets present at six other industrial clusters his expedition visited on a sort of whirlwind tour. Those items he could retrieve ended up in use at the Royal Aircraft Establishment (RAE) base at Farnborough, Britain's most important military aeronautics facility. Nevertheless, the British benefited less than either the Americans or Soviets from the process of claiming Germany's technical treasures as war reparations and/or plunder.

The reason for Britain's failure to exploit the situation more effectively lay in its own leadership rather than actual conditions on the ground. The British controlled an area of defeated Germany approximately equal to the zones held by the Americans and Soviets; only the French controlled a relatively minor portion of German territory. However, the British leaders failed to listen to their scientists, expressing disbelief that the technology would be of any use now that the Allies had secured victory. A further blow to the English scientists' plans came when Winston Churchill, an avid technophile in his own eccentric fashion, suffered a startling electoral defeat, resulting in his replacement by Clement Atlee.

Stalin, for all his personal coarseness, recognized the power of technology to transform his paranoid, authoritarian country into a world power, and Harry S. Truman, the new president following the death of Franklin D. Roosevelt, possessed enough clear-sighted pragmatism to recognize both the value of Third Reich science and the imminent threat of the resurgent Soviet Union. Only Attlee and his cabinet overlooked a principle enunciated centuries before by samurai warlord Tokugawa Ieyasu: "After a victory, tighten your helmet cords." Attlee also showed startling naiveté in initial dealings with the USSR.

Moreover, British leadership also proved more hostile to the notion of using "imported" German talent than the Americans (who offered the Germans various incentives) or the Soviets (who offered the Germans they seized no choice but to cooperate). All too many of England's decision-makers agreed with Fedden's immediate superior, Sir Stafford Cripps, who declared, "One can only tolerate the Germans by squeezing their knowledge out of them as quickly as possible and then having nothing more to do with them." (Herwig, , 125).

Conversely, Fedden understood the situation and value of German intellectuals to the future of

British defense. Faced by the inaction of his superiors, he used his team to gather a group of potential recruits. However, this scheme ran afoul of the dilatory, reluctant decision-making of England's leadership, and the Germans either found themselves snapped up by the Soviets or turned to the Americans instead, prompting a bitter commentary from the 60-year-old knight: "I collected a team of German jet engine specialists, who I felt would be invaluable to our country, but the delays after I had flown home to consult with the authorities about their disposition in Britain made them impatient. When I got back [...] The German specialists had been whisked away somewhere else, and were lost to us. Only Britain of the wartime 'Big Three' victors could not be bothered to appreciate the implications of the new aeronautical technique which Germany had assimilated." (Christopher, 2013, 278).

Despite these errors, the British did not walk away empty-handed. Though the Americans benefited most of all, England and the Soviet Union each made solid gains, and while the French controlled only a small portion of the destroyed Reich compared to the other Allied powers, Charles de Gaulle's newly minted government managed to secure a few juicy technological prizes for their nation.

One of the major prizes obtained from the Third Reich consisted of massive wind tunnels built to rigorously and effectively test new aircraft designs. Some of these constructions represented the largest, most precise wind tunnels in the world at the time. Removal of them to the victors' nations provided them with a ready-made means of testing the new aircraft their engineers developed based on German aerodynamics discoveries and jet engine research.

During the war, the Third Reich's scientists, pushing towards creation of supersonic interceptors, needed a wind tunnel capable of generating equivalently supersonic wind speeds. Only in this way could they conduct a fully realistic test of fighter aircraft and missiles under the stresses of supersonic flight. Thus, late in 1944, the Germans began construction of the supersonic wind tunnel near Ötztal, an Austrian city, under the codename "Zitteraal," or "Electric Eel." The Germans designed this tunnel to operate at 75 megawatts, pushing 10 tons of air per second through the 25-foot diameter tunnel to achieve a wind speed of Mach 1.

The Zitteraal tunnel, built by the usual sacrificial slave labor (mostly unfortunate Soviet soldiers), had not yet reached completion when the Allies took the region. The partially completed Ötztal facility lay in an area of Austria apportioned to the French, but its half-built condition created special problems for its new owners. Frank Wartendorf, a member of the U.S. scientific advisory team to Operation Overcast, Operation Paperclip, and similar operations, located many vital components on railcars in Stuttgart marked as "scrap steel" and successfully redirected them to a U.S. Army depot. Other parts remained at factories in the American zone, not yet shipped to Ötztal.

Under Wartendorf's urging, the Americans drove a shrewd bargain in exchange for releasing the vital components – needed to complete the Ötztal wind tunnel – to the French. The French granted the Americans the right to study the tunnel's entire design, and also to conduct tests in it later, on favorable terms. Part of this 1946 agreement reads, "[T]o admit to the French, American representatives to technical data including drawings for transmittal to Wright Field and to technical installations for inspection in all French zones. Of particular and of immediate interest in this connection are […] all of the design, construction and operational information concerning the Oetztal tunnel." (Hiebert, 2012, 290).

With their own interests thus secured, the Americans handed over all the parts of the Ötztal "Zitteraal" tunnel in their possession. The French chose Modane as the site for the wind tunnel's new Gallic home. Its mountainous terrain in the Rhone-Alpes area provides the necessary hydraulic power to run the Ötztal tunnel.

The Zitteraal became the centerpiece of Modane's ONERA (Office National d'Etudes et de Recherches Aérospatiales) facility, and remains operational as of 2016. The tunnel is powered by generators developing 88 megawatts of power, rather than the original 75 megawatts, and provides testing conditions from Mach 0.05 to Mach 1. Many French aircraft have undergone testing in the transplanted Ötztal tunnel, including the Mirage series of jet fighters, various Airbus designs, and the famous Concorde.

Chapter 6: The Soviet Union's Acquisition Efforts

Due to the speed and force of the final American drive into Germany, U.S. soldiers occupied many areas designated as Soviet zones at Yalta. Some of the soldiers and commanders expressed disgust at abandoning this territory to the Soviets after fighting to secure it, but the Western Allies adhered to the letter, if not the spirit, of their agreements. Nevertheless, the Americans removed as much scientific material (and as many scientists) as possible from these zones during their brief occupation.

The Soviets' own scientific teams often found the regions picked bare of technological prizes once the Americans vacated them, but the USSR did not come away empty-handed. The Soviets, in fact, carried out a similar stripping of American sectors in reverse when they took Berlin. The Kaiser Wilhelm Society Institute for Physics, its director Peter Adolf Thiessen, and a number of its scientists fell into Soviet hands. The Red Army's scientific teams, equivalent to the western T-Forces, also managed to secure many chemical, biochemical, and silicate research labs plus their personnel in the Berlin area.

The bribes brought by these teams added a bizarre touch to the proceedings: "The dismantlers showed up at the institutes with vodka and lard: vodka for the local military commandants, whose cooperation was necessary for quickly transporting the labs, lard for the German scientists, to convince them that the Soviets were serious about taking care of them." (Naimark, 1995, 209).

The Soviets, knowing that the Americans would permit the German scientists to leave if they wished to, attempted to take advantage of the much more liberal U.S. attitude towards the Third Reich's inventors and engineers. During the interrogation of these individuals at sites in Germany and in Paris during summer 1945, the various Allies naturally had the right to send their own representatives to the interviews, so the Soviet interrogators approached the German scientists with smoothly plausible claims, offering them considerable rewards and promising they could conduct their research in Germany.

Von Braun and most of the other scientists politely declined these offers, knowing them to be outright lies and fearing what the Soviets would do if they voluntarily joined those of their peers already captured by the Red Army. Helmut Gröttrup, however, naively believed the Soviets' blandishments, and the Americans, in keeping with their general policy, allowed him to leave. As soon as Gröttrup reached the Soviet-controlled area of Germany, however, he found himself bundled onto a train with his wife and other high-value scientists and their families. Under guard, the Germans traveled to remote sites in Siberia, where they spent years imprisoned (albeit well-fed and kept relatively comfortable). Von Braun noted that the Russians "let them see nothing, touch nothing on the production end, learn nothing from developing experience, just had them write reports until they were drained dry. Then the Russians went on by themselves." (Spangenburg, 2008, 79).

The Soviets also bagged the famous Gustav Hertz, taking him and the entire Siemens laboratory to Moscow. General A.P. Zaveniagin headed the collection of German atomic scientists still present in Russian-occupied territories and their organization into a useful program. While none of the scientists suffered direct mistreatment – in fact, the Soviets attended assiduously to their health and general well-being to ensure they did not lose the services of these valuable individuals through illness – most found themselves trapped in what amounted to comfortable prisons in the USSR.

While the Soviets simply arrested and deported some of the scientists – typically taking their families along to serve both as hostages and to make the men's captivity more bearable (and thus more productive) – they also used outright reassuring lies to lure many of the scientists into coming voluntarily to Russia for a "brief stay" that proved anything but short. As Manfred von Ardenne, a cyclotron designer, and his wife recounted, "With relatively light hearts, we left the children and everything else behind in Lichterfeld because we had gone for a two-week trip to the Soviet Union 'only to conclude a contract.' Those two weeks turned into ten years." (Naimark, 1995, 210).

Hertz

Once in Russia, most of the scientists received no release to return to their homes in Germany for 10 years, with many returns permitted in 1955. Even those few scientists actually interned by the Western Allies, by contrast, typically found themselves back in Germany (if they did not wish to remain in a different country) by 1948.

Zaveniagin, a man of scientific bent, continued to run the German science assets in the Soviet Union. However, other men joined him, including the sinister Lavrenty Beria, a sexual predator, rapist, and serial killer whose "peccadilloes" met with little more than amusement when Stalin learned of them. Beria oversaw the infamous Semipalatinsk nuclear testing ground in Kazakhstan, which witnessed nearly 500 nuclear tests prior to its closure by Nursultan Nazarbayev, Kazakhstan's current president for life, in 1991.

Beria

The Soviets also made rocket advances using material recovered from Mittelwerke – mostly machinery too heavy for the Americans to remove. Valentin Glushko headed the scientific investigation of the A-4/V-2 rocket and the initial Russian rocket program based upon it. However, the rocket program in Germany proper only lasted until late 1946.

At that point, Beria sent his lieutenant, Colonel-General Serov, to carry out Operation Osoaviakhim, named for a former Soviet paramilitary aviation organization's acronym. Units of Russian military police and soldiers swarmed into Berlin on October 22nd and carried out relatively peaceful but forcible deportation of thousands of German scientists, technicians, engineers, toolmakers, and their families. One witness reported, "In the dwellings of the families involved, the wardrobes were immediately nailed shut, and guards posted until a Russian truck and several Russian soldiers arrived who loaded all the inventory and the family (from the grandfather to the baby) and took them to the railway stations […] Everything was carried off, including cabinets, china, carpets, chairs, pianos, bird cages, and I even saw stove pipes." (Naimark, 1995, 220).

The Soviets also removed the contents of laboratories and factories, and then, in some cases, they dynamited the empty buildings. Similar deportations occurred throughout East Germany simultaneously. While the Russians picked the men carefully, they tended to seize any young woman nearby on the assumption she was the German's wife, leading to some German workers being deported along with maids, secretaries, or female cleaning staff. In some cases, local Soviet military governors protested, but Beria's will overrode them, as did the swarms of NKVD agents (the Soviet's Gestapo) and special troop detachments sent to assist with Osoaviakhim.

In some factories, German workers tried to flee, leading to NKVD men chasing them down and beating them into submission (or unconsciousness) with clubs, then dragging their inert forms to the waiting trucks. Once aboard the trains, the Soviets forced the Germans to sign three, five, or ten year contracts to work in the Soviet Union.

The deportation took place on a massive scale, with approximately 15,000 German scientists and technicians seized, plus tens of thousands of their relatives. The haul in material represented an even larger quantity, with the Zeiss plant in Jena alone stripped of all but 582 of its 10,000 manufacturing machines. The Soviets also carried out later, smaller sweeps to collect military specialists.

As fate had it, these German scientists themselves made only a modest contribution to Russia's first successful nuclear bomb test in 1949. The bulk of the success stemmed from espionage (obtaining American nuclear secrets) combined with Soviet scientists using the theoretical work written by the Germans during World War II.

Moreover, for years following Operation Osoaviakhim, the Soviets found it extremely difficult to coax their East German subjects into engineering or science, as the Germans feared being forcibly deported in the same manner. The Soviet rocket program, nylon manufacture, advanced fuels, and many other fields received an immense boost from the efforts of the men removed to the USSR during Osoaviakhim.

Chapter 7: Operation Paperclip

Operation Paperclip represented the successor to Operation Overcast. The Americans spearheaded this effort to recruit the Reich's scientists, simultaneously putting their formidable intellectual prowess at the service of the free world and keeping them out of the clutches of the Soviets. Its prosaic name derived from the equally prosaic paperclips used to hold documents together in the U.S. Army's files on leading German experts.

While the immense tonnage of documents, plus various experimental test models of advanced aircraft, and the V-2 rockets themselves, constituted a priceless haul of booty, the Allies considered the "human capital" gained in the persons of the scientists themselves even more valuable. These men, after all, already knew how to use the research material, served as living indexes for it, and could reconstruct gaps in the information caused by accidental or deliberate destruction during the war.

The German scientists interviewed by the Western Allies at this time understood the political situation and their potential fates quite quickly, despite Third Reich efforts to demonize the Western Allies in addition to the Soviets. The advancing Soviets, in fact, carried on a campaign of murder, torture, rapine, and pillage that nearly equaled the blackest imaginings of Goebbels' propaganda bureaus, and the Germans, understanding this and knowing the Anglo-Americans to be relatively merciful despite their fierce determination to achieve victory, frequently fled westward in vast numbers to avoid falling into the area controlled by Stalin's predatory armies: "[T]he mission believes that the engineers, technicians, and executives who were interrogated [...] wished to be helpful [...] It was sensed that there was considerable apprehension on the part of the German scientists and engineers as to their future. Several spoke of their desire to move their staffs and equipment to America or particularly to Canada." (Christopher, 2013, 80).

Following the attack on Peenemunde as part of Operation Crossbow, Heinrich Himmler had managed to gain control over the much-coveted A-4 rocket program, dislodging it from the grip of the Luftwaffe. Even as the war continued to go poorly, the various Nazi organizations tore at each other in a savage attempt to win a little extra power and influence within the crumbling Reich. In order to assert his dominance over the rocket scientists, Himmler ordered von Braun's arrest, and that of several of his colleagues, on vague, trumped-up charges. Held in SS cells for two weeks, the men emerged with no doubt of their master's identity.

Himmler

Himmler subsequently placed SS officer Hans Kammler at the head of the A-4/V-2 program. Kammler, a handsome man with a face disfigured by a permanent sneer of cold aggression, ran the rocketry program ruthlessly, making heavy use of slave labor. At the war's end, he concocted a scheme to possibly save his own skin. On April 1st, 1945, Kammler collected 500 of the leading Third Reich scientists, including von Braun, and sent them to Oberammergau, 400 miles to the south in the Bavarian Alps. While he told the scientists his intention was to fight on from the "Alpine Redoubt," using their research services, Kammler actually intended to use them as bargaining chip; he would trade the 500 scientists to the Americans for his own life and freedom after his numerous, appalling war crimes. When von Braun and his fellow experts reached Oberammergau, they found themselves herded into a barbed wire enclosure and guarded by a detachment of fanatical, heavily armed SS, rather more as prisoners than scientists preparing to create new wonder weapons for an eleventh-hour Third Reich victory.

Kammler

When Kammler arrived several weeks later, he called von Braun to a conference at the local tavern. The rocket scientist found the SS man, whose thugs held him and his fellows prisoner, oddly conciliatory, albeit unwilling to release the 500 men from the compound. Secretly, von Braun feared that Kammler meant to use them as hostages, or even massacre them to deny the Allies their intellectual capital.

After his talk with von Braun, Kammler left Oberammergau, saying he would return soon. In fact, he never did, and his day of departure represented the last confirmed sighting of the SS officer. Kammler's exact fate remains mysterious. Several people, including his wife, claimed that he committed suicide with cyanide capsules rather than fall into Allied hands and answer for his war crimes. Some of these accounts report seeing his corpse without specifying the cause of death. Other reported fates for Kammler include death during a gun-battle in Prague, during which 500 Czech resistance fighters finally overwhelmed and killed 21 heavily armed SS men, including Kammler; escape to the United States as part of the Paperclip program; a similar story in which the Americans imprisoned Kammler in a subterranean cell until he hanged himself in despair; and entry into Soviet service alongside other former Third Reich personnel involved with the V-2 rocket program.

Either way, the scientists felt nothing but relief at the cunning, deadly Kammler's departure. Von Braun soon talked the junior SS officer left in charge, Sturmbannführer (Major) Kummer, a polite and rather mild-mannered fellow for a member of the *Schutzstaffel*, into letting the scientists out of their close confinement.

All the while, von Braun, with his left arm and shoulder in a cast due to an accidental break in a car crash, continued to plan for the scientists' safety. The men conferred among themselves about which Allied power represented their best bet for future research opportunities (and basic survival). One of them later summed up the deliberations pragmatically: "We despise the French, we are mortally afraid of the Soviets, we don't believe the British can afford us, so that leaves the Americans." (Spangenburg, 2008, 77).

On April 25th, Walter Dornberger, von Braun's former overseer at Peenemunde, unexpectedly turned up with 100 Wehrmacht soldiers. He extracted von Braun and took him to a resort hotel in Hindelang held by his men. There, von Braun met his younger brother Magnus, and heard from Dornberger how he had invited one of the SS officers to drink with him. Kammler's parting orders had been, in fact, to execute all 500 scientists as soon as the Americans or French put in an appearance. Dornberger succeeded in disarming the SS detachment by offering them Wehrmacht uniforms, which would prevent their being shot out of hand by vengeful Allied soldiers (though many SS soldiers were able to surrender successfully at the war's end).

In this remote location, Dornberger, von Braun, the scientists, and the soldiers waited to see what fate would bring them. The news of Adolf Hitler's death galvanized von Braun with fresh resolve to reach the United States and carry on his research, which Dornberger seconded. Dornberger himself reflected on the surreal peace of their surroundings while the waiting continued: "About us towered the snow-covered Allgau mountains, their peaks glittering in the sunlight under the clear blue sky. Far below us it was already spring. The hill pastures were a bright green. Even on our high mountain pass the first flowers were thrusting buds through the melting snow. Had the last few years been nothing but a bad dream?" (McGovern, 1964, 140).

Finally, the U.S. Seventh Army moved against the "Alpine Redoubt," finding only scattered Wehrmacht units rather than a formidable mountain fastness. An anti-tank battalion of the 324th Infantry Regiment moved along a road near Hindelang and, on a misty day, encountered a lone young man on a bicycle. A soldier from Sheboygan, Wisconsin, Private First Class (PFC) Fred Schneiker, met him and discovered him to be Magnus von Braun. The Americans disbelieved Magnus' story at first but brought him to the local Counterintelligence Command (CIC) HQ.

Eventually, he convinced the American intelligence personnel. Wernher von Braun and his leading scientists made their way nervously to Reutte, escorted by Jeeps. Rather than being "kicked in the teeth," as von Braun had feared, the Germans underwent an ordinary debriefing, followed by billeting in local houses and an American breakfast of fried eggs the following morning. The Americans moved the 500 scientists to Garmisch and temporarily interned them there for questioning about the V-2 rockets. The vast majority of the men received their release from custody within 2 weeks or less.

Meanwhile, U.S. Colonel Holger N. Toftoy spearheaded the effort of the Americans to bring the German scientists to America. The Germans and Americans bargained, and as part of the deal they worked out, U.S. teams located the families of the scientists and brought them to Landshut. There they received food, clothing, and shelter while awaiting transport to America along with those of the scientists who chose to emigrate there. Toftoy's agents even managed to extract most of the families located behind Soviet lines through what he described as "cloak and dagger methods."

Toftoy

The Americans "loaned" their newly acquired scientists to Britain for two weeks, during which time the English tried to persuade them to remain in the UK rather than traveling to the U.S. Their efforts proved vain, however. Most of the Germans remained determined to travel to

America, which they believed had the resources to carry out their rocketry dreams and the strength to emerge victorious in a future clash with the Soviets. In one case, the Americans handed over Walter Dornberger to the British for war crimes trial, and after the court eventually acquitted him in 1947, the general traveled to join the rest of the Peenemunde men in their new western hemisphere homeland.

With the German scientists willing – and in some cases eager – to leave war-ravaged, Soviet-threatened Germany for the New World, the U.S. Army flew a select few to Boston in September 1945. The rest followed by ship in November of the same year. From the East Coast, the Germans traveled to El Paso, Texas by railway. Von Braun found himself amazed at the gigantic spaces of the United States.

The initial group of German scientists permitted into the country numbered 118. However, the Paperclip project expanded as it started yielding scientific dividends, and America eventually brought 700 experts to its shores, plus their families. For years, much of the research occurred in the southwest, with V-2 rockets and other devices tested at White Sands. Many of the Germans adopted "western" fashion, wearing cowboy hats or sombreros along with cowboy boots.

Tests of the V-2 rocket began at White Sands in May 1946, with the first successful launch in June. The Germans worked to teach the American rocketry scientists what they knew. The once-terrifying V-2s now carried scientific instruments for studying the planet's upper atmospheric layers, providing an additional layer of usefulness.

Wernher von Braun and other scientists first entered the United States as special employees of the U.S. Army. However, the INS (Immigration and Naturalization Service) objected to this, declaring the Germans to be illegal immigrants. To solve the problem, the Army engaged in a piece of border theater of a type familiar to anyone who has traveled extensively between countries. The Army drove the Germans to El Paso, Texas, and there the group of scientists crossed the bridge to Juarez, on Mexican territory. There, they boarded a streetcar and crossed into the United States again, where border agents officially prepared their entry papers as legal immigrants. Von Braun later relished describing the event: "On my immigration papers, [...] where the 'Vessel of Entry' column normally would have a romantic name such as 'Queen Mary' or 'Isle de France' or 'Mayflower,' it states: 'Entered at El Paso, Texas – via Streetcar!' [...] We called it our 'Streetcar named Desire.' The fare was five cents, and it was the most valuable nickel I have ever spent." (Ward, 2005, 74).

With the Germans now officially immigrants and able to stay indefinitely in the United States, the door opened for more complex experiments. At this point, the American government temporarily lost interest in their coterie of German scientists, atleast until the 1949 Soviet atom bomb test shocked them out of their torpor. With a new sense of urgency, the Americans moved the scientists to the newly constituted Redstone Arsenal in northern Alabama, close to

Huntsville. While the Germans continued their work and the Americans joined in, Wernher von Braun performed an additional service. With his optimistic, outgoing personality and superb "people skills," he tirelessly promoted space exploration and aerospace research to the American public. This soon made it far easier to secure funding for space programs, as did the partnership offered by Walt Disney, who added "Tomorrowland" to Disney World in honor of the German scientist's achievements and vision, which impressed him vastly.

Though the top scientists in von Braun's group of 500 represented the centerpiece of Operation Paperclip, the U.S. Army's intelligence units also located thousands of additional scientists and technicians elsewhere, including 4,500 housed in the villages near Mittelwerke and awaiting their fate as the Allied juggernaut rolled over Germany. The U.S. Third Armored Division stumbled upon the Mittelwerke facility, still intact and with its lighting and ventilation operational. Realizing the treasure they had located, they communicated the find of this "magician's cave" to headquarters.

The men also found the horrors of the Nordhausen and Dora concentration camps, filled with shambling, skeletal prisoners and reeking heaps of corpses. With pitiful enthusiasm, five of the nearly-dead prisoners attempted to hoist the commander of the first American tank to drive into the camp, Lt. Herbert Gontard, onto their shoulders but collapsed under his weight. Filled with rage, the American soldiers turned the camps over to doctors and support troops, then hurled themselves into battle with the next Wehrmacht units with fresh motivation: "[T]he tankers of the 3rd were in a savage mood as they went on to the final battles." (McGovern, 1964, 122).

They had, however, secured one of the largest troves of surviving V-2 technology for the U.S. The intelligence troops of Toftoy found 100 disassembled V-2 rockets in the facility. Nearby, the bombing of bridges had trapped hundreds of German rail cars very close to Mittelwerke. Delighted by these finds, the Americans loaded the V-2 rockets onto the rail cars, repaired the railroad bridges, and shipped the rockets to Antwerp.

At Antwerp, the British protested, asking the Americans to hand over half of the V-2 rockets. Colonel Joel Holmes of the Technical Division took advantage of the red tape involved in launching such a protest. He shipped the V-2s to the U.S. as soon as they could be loaded, so that by the time the order to split the rockets with the English arrived, the weapons were well on their way to American shores. Holmes received a tongue-lashing for his actions, but he took this calmly in stride as a trivial price to pay for the extra rockets. These rockets eventually ended up at White Sands for Von Braun's team to use. The Americans also ferreted out and retrieved the enormous cache of 14 tons of documents placed in the mine by Huzel at von Braun's request.

Though the controversy over bringing Third Reich scientists to the United States never died – and, indeed, periodically resurrects thanks to newly published books on the topic – Operation Paperclip yielded undoubted benefits to the U.S. and the entire free world. The creation of the atom bomb and its eventual union with the ballistic missile – the synthesis of

American and German World War II science – created a situation in which global war paradoxically became less, rather than more, likely.

For decades, the Soviet Union continued to probe for advantage, seeking to expand its empire into Western Europe through various abortive communist movements. The United States and the USSR arguably fought World War III during the years described as the "Cold War," with the Soviets mostly acting through proxies such as the North Koreans and North Vietnamese. America, in turn, funded the resistance against Soviet aggression in Afghanistan and supported Israel against Soviet-backed Arab states in the strategically crucial oil lands of the Middle East. These proxy wars tested the Americans' resolve and also sought to undermine or bolster political support for a free world united against the "red fascism" of the USSR. That the scattered conflicts and "brushfire wars" never coalesced into a global cataclysm like World War II, in which the Warsaw Pact and NATO went head to head in Europe and likely on every other continent, may well have resulted from the threat of mutually assured destruction presented by the nuclear ballistic missile.

Thus, it's fair to assert that the nuclear-armed descendants of Wernher von Braun's A-4 rockets kept the lid on the Pandora's Box of a planet-wide conventional war of apocalyptic proportions, thus leading to the eventual withering of the inefficient, despotic Soviet system and the slow, painful, but quickening spread of democracy and human rights to many other regions of the world.

Operation Paperclip also paved the way for a peaceful application for Wernher von Braun's technology – indeed, that which first captured his enthusiasm in the days between the World Wars. The first tentative but critical ventures of humanity into space, including the Apollo Mission, the satellite network, the space shuttle, and various scientific probes, emerged from the technological treasures and intellectual prowess gained for the United States through Paperclip. Walter Dornberger offered an insightful commentary following one of the A-4 rocket's early launches: "We have invaded space with our rocket, and for the first time—mark this well—have used space as a bridge between two points on Earth; we have proved rocket propulsion practicable for space travel. To land, sea, and air may now be added infinite empty space as an area of future transportation, that of space travel." (Spangenburg, 2008, 56).

The 21st century entrepreneur and space enthusiast Elon Musk compared the first trip into space as being as important to the history of life on Earth as the first animal venturing forth onto land out of the sea. While Robert Goddard built the first liquid-fuel rocket, the Germans of Operation Paperclip brought a critical element to the United States – their fascination with space and belief in the value of interplanetary exploration. Despite the dark past of Third Reich science, Paperclip brought the German and American scientists of the mid-20th century together to launch the Space Age, a towering breakthrough which someday may be universally recognized as having the same importance as the evolution of land animals, or the first use of fire or the wheel.

Online Resources

Other World War II titles by Charles River Editors

Other titles about Operation Paperclip on Amazon

Bibliography

Christopher, John. *The Race for Hitler's X-Planes: Britain's 1945 Mission to Capture Secret Luftwaffe Technology*. Stroud, 2013.

Goudsmit, Samuel A. *Alsos*. Woodbury, 1996.

Herwig, Dieter and Heinz Rode. *Luftwaffe Secret Projects: Strategic Bombers 1935-1945*. Earl Shilton, 2000.

Hiebert, David M. "Air Engineering Development Center: Part I – Rising From the Ashes of World War II." *ITEA Journal*, 33, 2012, pp. 287-293.

McGovern, James. *Crossbow and Overcast*. New York, 1964.

Naimark, Norman M. *The Russians in Germany: A History of the Soviet Zone of Occupation, 1945-1949*. Cambridge, 1995.

Neufeld, Michael J. *The Rocket and the Reich: Peenemunde and the Coming of the Ballistic Missile Era*. Washington, DC, 1995.

Ostyn, Charles. "Personal account" on *V2Rocket.com*, http://www.v2rocket.com/start/chapters/antwerp.html , retrieved April 6th, 2016.

Samuel, Wolfgang W.E. *American Raiders: The Race to Capture the Luftwaffe's Secrets*. Jackson,   2004.

Spangenburg, Ray and Diane Kit Moser. *Wernher von Braun: Rocket Visionary*. New York, 2008.

Stocker, Jeremy. *Britain and Ballistic Missile Defense 1942-2002*. New York, 2004.

Ward, Bob. *Dr. Space: The Life of Wernher von Braun*. Annapolis, 2005.

Zaloga, Steven. *V-2 Ballistic Missile, 1942-52*. Oxford, 2003.

Made in the USA
Monee, IL
23 March 2020